D1249494

Word Bird's
Shapes

The Child's World

Published in the United States of America by The Child's World®, Inc.
PO Box 326
Chanhassen, MN 55317-0326
800-599-READ
www.childsworld.com

Project Manager Mary Berendes
Editor Katherine Stevenson, Ph.D.
Designer Ian Butterworth

Library of Congress Cataloging-in-Publication Data
Moncure, Jane Belk.
Word Bird's shapes / by Jane Belk Moncure.
p. cm.
Summary: Word Bird makes objects of various shapes
while playing with his toys.
ISBN 1-56766-998-0 (lib. : alk. paper)
[1. Shape—Fiction. 2. Birds—Fiction.]   I. Title.
PZ7.M739 Wor 2002
[E]—dc21
2001006044

Word  Bird's™

Shapes

by Jane Belk Moncure

illustrated by Chris McEwan

Papa Bird gave
Word Bird a box
of squares. . .

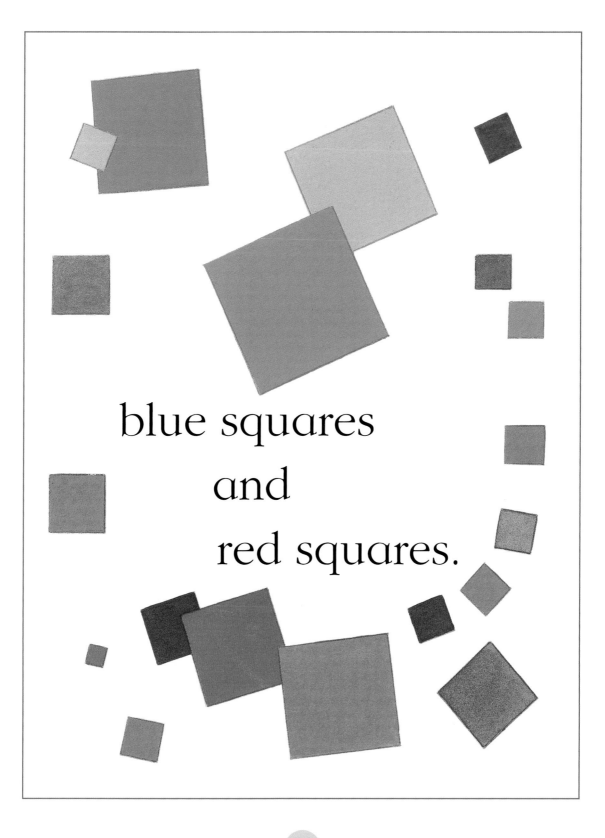

blue squares
and
red squares.

"I will make something
with my squares,"
Word Bird said.

Word Bird made
something square.

Mama Bird gave
Word Bird a box
of circles. . .

green circles

and

yellow circles.

"I will make something with my circles," Word Bird said.

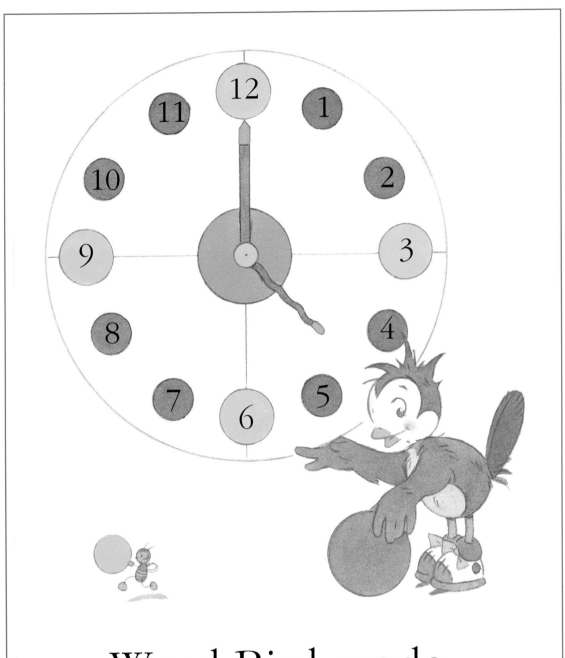

Word Bird made
something round.

Then Papa gave
Word Bird a box
of triangles. . .

orange triangles

and

purple triangles.

"I will make something
with my triangles,"
Word Bird said.

Word Bird made a
big triangle.

Then Mama gave
Word Bird a box of
rectangles. . .

pink
rectangles

and

brown
rectangles.

"I will make something
with my rectangles,"
Word Bird said.

This is what Word
Bird made.

Then Mama said,
"It is time to put your
shapes away."

Word Bird put the squares,
the circles,. . .

the triangles, and the
rectangles in boxes.

Then Word Bird tripped!

Squares,

circles,

triangles,

and rectangles

fell all over the floor.

"Look," said Papa. "Look
what you can make now."

"With all the shapes, you can make a train."

"You can also make

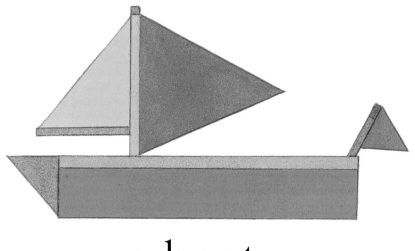

a boat,

a plane,

a rocket,

a tree,. . .

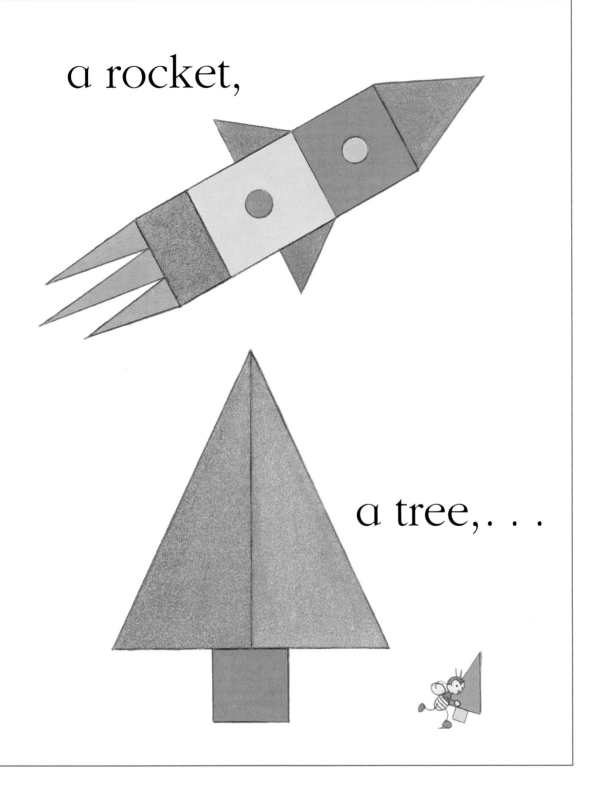

a toy teepee,

a house,

a hat,

a truck,

and a cat."

What else?

Can you read these words with Word Bird?

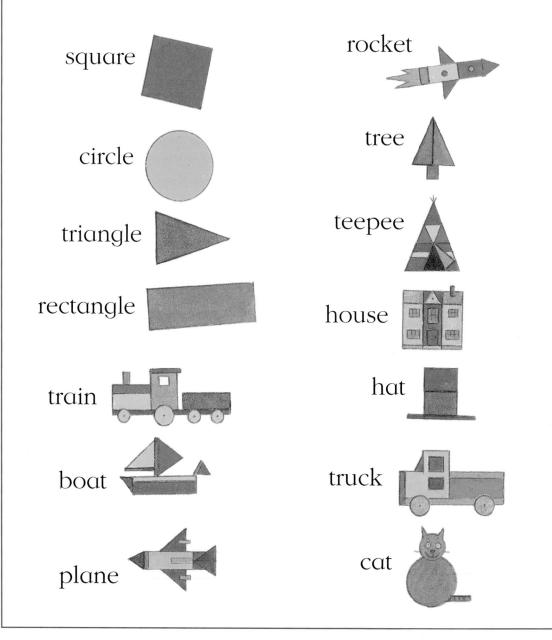

square

circle

triangle

rectangle

train

boat

plane

rocket

tree

teepee

house

hat

truck

cat